IDYLLIC

Very pleasant and peaceful; perfect

Acknowledgement

Writing this collection of poems has been deeply a personal journey and I am grateful to everyone who has supported me along the way. I extend my gratitude to my family for their patience and understanding during the writing process. Your support has been a source of strength and comfort. I want to thank VANYAA and BHAVYA, their unwavering encouragement and insightful feedback were invaluable. Your belief in this project kept me motivated and inspired.

This book is a piece of my heart and I'm honored to share it with you.

Dear Reader,

Consider this book as my personal diary. Each and every poem has a part of me. The best way to enjoy this book is reading one page per day.

Have a happy reading.

The way nature screams,
It calms my soul
The sound of thunder
always made me wonder
Why don't I show emotions
Sometimes even the sky is in commotion
It's weird,
the thoughts in my mind were cleared
by the thunder and rain
it eliminated my pain.
A lull before Gale
As we reach in a fairytale
I don't know why
it feels like a lie
people being petrified from thunder
is a big blunder
it's my wish, before I die
I want to see the thunder in the sky.
Feeling of torrential rain
made me overlook my pain
it is a way nature express
all the pain and it's stress
My love for Gale
Always feels like a fairytale

Sitting on my chair
Trying to find a rhyming pair
A sudden burst of thoughts came crashing
The moments of love kept flashing

Listening to music while writing
The poem and my thoughts kept fighting
It's raining outside
Which makes the chaos in me so quite

My Mumma preparing a delicious tea,
The squirrels dancing on a beautiful tree
It's not just a downpour
But for all my worries and stress, it's a cure

OMG! The smell of rain
Its like a drug for my pain
Rain, music and journal is all I require
To achieve a peaceful mindset, which I have always desired.

People say they know me very well
But they need to understand that it is a mystic spell
How can someone know me
When they never saw me cry
how can someone know me
When they don't know why my eyes are dry

How can someone know me
When they never saw me dance
How can someone know me
When they don't know why do I always fall into a trance

How can someone know me
When they don't know why I embrace silence
How can someone know me
When they don't know my life's sequence

Trust me, it's a mystic spell
To think that you know me very well
You only know what I show
Cause I like to keep my life a little bit low

Life is neither fixed nor absolute, it's ambiguous
But still we humans are clueless,
Clueless about its possibilities entailed by existence
To know about life one has to travel a certain
distance.

Life is both sadness and beatitude
One way to live it blissfully is through gratitude
Life is not just a four letter word
But it tells us to go with the flow, just like a bird

Life is both destruction and creation
It's about celebrating birth and cremation
Life is finding a cause to survive
It's an ocean in which you've to dive.

For some life is creating happiness
For some life is a huge mess.
It's you who has to decide,
For you, What is Life?

It's 7:00 am, sitting in the lobby
observing people is my favorite hobby.
It took sometime but soon I realized,
In railway stations, you'll see one of the hardest goodbyes.

People starting a new chapter,
Students coming home after an end of a semester
Parents with a heavy heart send their children,
Tears behind their eyes are hidden.

A father giving a hug to his daughter
A boy taking blessings from his mother
You can see different types of emotions,
From sadness to joyful expressions.

I guess that's how life is,
With goodbyes, sadness and bliss.
This is what I observed,
All the emotions of people that are preserved.

I have letters to write but not words to explain
Left with nothing to lose and don't want anything to gain.
They say I'm overthinking
But they don't realize the boat of my life is sinking.

Some days I just want to disappear
Putting a final end to all my grief and fear
It's funny, even the people close to me
Don't even realize I'm drowning in the mysticism of sea.

I'm ready to take responsibility of my actions,
But what about those souls who are creating a distraction.
My life is no more about me
It's about the baffling things that I see.

'MAYAA' is everything they believe
But beyond MAYAA is a mysterious world only few could see.
In this world I'm all alone,
Trying to fight those who are still unknown.

Everything happens for a reason,
But what's the reason behind someone drinking poison
Maybe he was killed mentally
The reason he wanted to demolish his presence physically.
Okay, I'm not promoting suicide
Life and death are the two things that we divide
But don't you think that's a murder
Committed either physically or mentally of every suicider.
Sometimes I think, which incident triggered him
What forced him to take that step when light was dim.
Maybe he was in a lot of pain
Maybe he thought there was nothing left for him to gain.
Don't get me wrong, I'm not promoting it in any way
But don't you think it's unfair to just assume and say
Don't you think we should listen, what he has to say
Why no one could save him in every possible way.

What do you love? He asked
I don't know what I love! I exclaimed
Guess I never payed attention to me
Always waited for someone in this huge crowd,
who could see me.

Yes, I don't talk, I embrace silence
It was a choice? No, it was a test of my patience.
Maybe one day I'll find someone
To whom I can rant about anything and anyone.

One day, my life will be no more about others
It'll be about the things that I love, just like
feathers.
One day someone will understand my silence and
tranquil
This time the spark in me will enlighten and anxiety
is what I'll kill.

Yesterday , when it was 2 am
I heard him scream my name
The scream which was filled with agony
Didn't realize he lived in his own type of
melancholy.

It was too much for me
Hearing from things which you can't even see
Why does it happen? I don't know
But it is something, I don't want to show.

Even the winds were not able to tell
How did he became so unwell
Even the clouds were peeping
When they heard him screaming.

It's a mystery for the time
But soon I'll unravel this crime
For the time being, let's name him UNKNOWN
MR UNKNOWN who likes to live alone.

To that feminine energy who always protected me
From the energies that only I used to see
Whenever I was lost and felt scared
You were the only one who always cared.

Some days I was stubborn and would fight
But you never left me from your sight.
The one holding my hand and would help me walk
Walk through the toughest paths, about which no one used to talk.

Me crying myself to bed
You were the one who used to caress my head
You're the divine still you care for me
The one who pulled me out when I was drowning in the sea.

Maa DURGA , I bow down to you
The miracles that you did only few knew
Thank you for being the best
The one who made me forget about the rest.

Some scenes are quiet
Just like the solitude of sky at night,
The night where only few are awake
Some of them waiting for sun to wake.

It's about the mysticism of darkness
Where few people are afraid, you'll find your
consciousness.
Though some days you'll be unconscious
The time when GOD wants you to be cautious

The time which is a delusion
All of us are trapped in it's illusion
The delusion that only serpents know,
Mystery of serpents only conscious would know.

Cosmic nature of serpents
The seven chakras which they represent.
It's a mystery that Yogis used to believe
The mystery that only few could achieve.

Standing in the balcony
Thinking about few aspects of agony
Suddenly my eyes fell on a toddler
Smiling and talking to her grandfather.

Seeing her, my all thoughts started vanishing
But few memories came down crashing
Grandpa surprising me with sweets
Halloween with him was full of trick and treats.

Why can't these happy moments remain the same?
Why life always has to pay the price of pain?
I miss those old days,
When grandparents try their best to make you
happy in every possible ways.

I guess that's how life is
Not stopping for anything you miss.
Still grateful for those memories that were created
The memories from which you can never be
separated.

The comforting soul in the family
Her feelings can be delicate just like a water lily
The one who converts a house into a sweet home
The one who told me, in sky o dreams feel free to roam.
Standing in front of her family like a protective shield
No negative aura can enter in her protective field
The one who is a true meaning of love in herself
In order to protect her family, she sacrifices herself.
When you're unwell or when you start to weep
She'll always be there, even if it means sacrificing her sleep
Working hard everyday just to make you smile
Never asks for appreciation, not even once in a while.
I guess, now you understand who she is
A daughter, sister or wife but above all, the best MUMMA she is.
The comfort you'll find while talking to your mother
Best bond you can attain, is with your mother.

He is the one, who doesn't know how to express
Neither his love nor his stress
For me, he's a HERO without mask
For him, making me smile is an easy task.

He is one of the most dedicated man
Achieving everything with his support? Of course I
can
He is the one who inspires deeply
And the one who spoils me secretly.

All the sweetest things he do for me
Trust me, he makes the most delicious tea
Without him I'm nothing
Roasting others with him is my favorite thing.

I'm grateful to have you DAD
The one who can never see me sad
I never say I love you, just like the rest
But trust me DAD you're the best.

It’s fear I guess
Which has turned my life into such a mess.
Fear of not being perfect
Or the fear of not answering correct

The feeling that people are judging you
Sudden attacks of anxiety that no one knew
Maybe it’s just my mind
But comfort in people is hard to find.

‘FEAR’ just a four letter word, has a huge impact
Constant staring of people is like a harmful attack
It’s difficult to move out of comfort zone
But the fear that damages you, should be thrown.

Maybe life out of comfort zone is better
But moving out requires a huge courage to gather.
All you need is to believe in yourself, they say
Maybe it’s an only option to find our way.

Respect your work, home and school
Making fun of them, trust me you're a fool
This quote is what she told
Gradually realizing about the worth it hold.

She was teaching about the gratitude we need
Learning gratitude is like sowing a new seed.
This quote is like a stepping stone for me
I bet, how right was she

It was Saturday morning, you see
Sitting on first bench alone, not so difficult for me
The way she explained Gratitude,
The reason why I admire her positive attitude.

I bet no book can ever teach
The depths that experience can reach
It's a lesson I wanted to share,
Because lesson kept within is not so fair.

When you feel helpless
It's time for you to enter into a spiritual
consciousness
To be with the divine
For dark phases of your life, he's like a sunshine.

I know it's hard to move on
The pain in you will be long gone,
Once you hold his hand
His mysticism will save you from quick sand.

The faith and belief is all you need
You just have to sow a spiritual seed
It's not about you, praying everyday
But to turn your life in such a blissful way.

Some sense of gratitude is required
To live a blissful life that you've always desired
The gratitude towards nature or mother earth
For all the gifts that she gave you since birth.

Sitting on Ghats of KASHI
My body felt a little bit washy,
Started to think about the two aspects
A joyful life and embracing death.

Such a beautiful place KASHI is
Embracing Death? Never thought about this
People from around the world come to visit
And souls find their way of exit.

KASHI in itself is Divine
But the darkest scenes are hidden behind the
sunshine
The scenes of YATANA and the cosmic nature
Surrounded my mother Ganga is one of its feature.

Considered as the City Of Light
The mystic scenes of Manikarnika Ghat at night
Both cries and prayers are hard to forget,
Seeing it's cosmic nature might change your
mindset

Suddenly it became hard to breathe with racing heartbeat
Atmosphere of that room was boiling heat.
What was happening with me was hard to know
Because of the emotions that I don't used to show.

Then she grabbed my arm
As it was getting difficult for me to stay calm
It was getting hard to explain or say
But she handled me in the best possible way.

Definitely she proved her point of being the greatest friend
Panic attacks can give you the experience your end
I guess it's the first time when someone saw me like this
It's hard to live all the time in pure form of bliss.

It's a day, experience and a feeling I'll never forget
Sitting beside her is something that I'll never regret
This is something that I wanted to share
About the scenes when life is not so fair.

And then it's my favorite person
Behind my happiness she was the reason
The reason who always wanted well of me
But I never liked the way you dispelled me.

Together we had so many plans
Without you, the world feels full of scams
Not a single day goes like this kind
Where you don't cross my mind.

It's funny but I still wait for your wish
On every birthday you were the first one to wish
Now nothing feels the same anymore
No festival can make me happy like before.

NANI, where did you go?
Leaving your favorite kid all alone
I still have so many achievements to show
My plans with you are now unknown.

Echoes of failure whispered
But her words of wisdom are what I heard
Fear of Failure was rigorous to handle
But the word ‘FOCUS’ made I easy to detangle

They say, a single spark can ignite a thousand stars
In same way, a single appreciation can heal a
thousand scars
That is what I learned from her
Her guidance made everything, a little brighter

Her presence created a sense of reverence
When lost, I found my way back through her
guidance
From her I learned the essence of gratitude
Her teachings were something, I’ve always valued.

Let me tell you,
Something only few knew
She is the girl with the prettiest smile
Understanding her, took a while
She's wild in front of her friends
Her love for Punjabi songs never ends
She is a problem dealer
And for me she is a healer
Her jokes are wild
But I admire her inner child.
Her birthday month is
Either August or December
Moments spend with her I'll always remember
To that girl,
You're like a Melo pearl
The rarest and hard to find
Trust me you are one of a kind.

There is a Punjabi saying that goes,
Pyaar Nu Sambhalo Jivein
Kirnaan Nu Sooraj Sambhaalda

Which means,
Nurture love, like the sun nurture it's rays
It is one of the beautiful phrase
Reading this made me realize,
The love in people eyes
The deep affection of sun
Towards it's rays
Felt like the sunshine won
The love that sun conveys.

Calmness of mind, the strongest weapon that one can attain
To earn that, there will be many things that you've to detain
It's not something that can be bought
To earn that, with chaos I had to fought

If you ask me, How is earned it?
It's a place, I never thought I'll fit
To be honest, calmness of mind is good in its place
But sometimes, even chaos wants it to be chased.

Excessive of anything, destroys you
Even calmness has its way to pacify you
I never thought I'll ever be this calm
Even after so many scars in my palm

At the end, I earned the peace and tranquil
Even though it was against my will
My will, to be seen and heard
My will, to live in present and not looking forward.

I miss you everyday
Seeing you as a morning ray
Nani Maa, I love you
Wish I could tell you,
I miss our evening tea
You and I talking about our love for sea
Do you still remember my dance?
Never thought, it was my last chance
The last chance to hug you
How important you're, only few knew
I still remember,
Promise I made you in December
The promise that I'll never be able to fulfill
No matter how much I earn from my skill
Maa you were my safe place
That no house can replace.

It healed a part of me,
The morning breeze
Watching the sunrise
Felt like a paradise

The feeling was surreal,
Of things that nature wanted to reveal
My inner child was healing
The nature knew with what I was dealing

The wind was telling,
About the clouds blessing
The squirrels were grooving
As the clouds were moving

The trees were gossiping
About the two birds hugging;
Nature has its own mellifluous tone
Whose magic is still unknown

I am known for unknown
Fighting battles on my own
Things that trigger my headache
Soon people realized I was never awake.

It's funny,
How people can be so dummy
Thinking they know me
But there's a part they'll hardly ever see

Being a mystery was never the choice
People hardly ever heard my voice
The calmness in me was so mean
That even chaos begged me to be seen

Why are you this way?
People always say
They don't realize the damage they did,
When I was the happiest little kid.

It was 24th MAY,
She was trying to find her way
Her way out of the dark
But it was difficult to find that spark.

She was searching for EVARA,
A Gift Of GOD
For her, everything felt like a fraud
She knew she was going to die
Her last wish, seeing thunder in the sky

Gradually her soul found its way
It rained heavily that day
It felt like she was finally free
From the curse that only she used to see

The chaos was now calm
People still rubbing her palm
Everyone was sobbing
Apparently no one knew, how much her heart was throbbing

I don't know who you are
Thinking about you hit me like a speeding car
You're a mystery I think
Why you help me, when I sink?

I never saw you
How you protect me, no one knew
I always have a vision of your eyes
That easily got me mesmerized

I don't believe in soulmate,
Yet it feels like, you're my fate
Wish I knew, who you are
Always trying to heal my scar

Wish we will meet someday soon
On a cold November noon
It's a past life regression, I guess
But how you know, I'm in such a mess?

In English we say, I'm gonna miss this class
But in poetry we say,

Gradually we realize, no one ever lies
When they say, time flies
It breaks my heart like a glass
Only few months left before leaving this class

It feels like yesterday she hugged me,
But it has been 3 months, you see
Maybe I'm afraid of leaving my comfort zone
Or the only zone which I have always known

How'll I manage without those girls
Who are like the rarest pearls
It feels like yesterday
When we were rejoicing at her house on a sunny day

I'll always think
When I'll feel lost and will sink
Think about the word FOCUS
That she says when her students get nervous

Her eye's hold something that wasn't hers
The only thing that she ever tried to find was
kindness in others
But do you think, eye's like hers are really
appreciated?
I guess, the kindness she was trying to find was
never created

She was a poem
A poem, I could never write
Even her silence had a rhythm
Though her life was filled with darkness, her
presence made everything bright

She was the girl that disappears
The one, lost in books of William Shakespeare's
Rather than speaking, she believed in writing
An escape from agony, a world that she was
creating

She had literature inside her heart
That she couldn't sometimes write
In abandoned things, she found art
Days were fine, but she always craved for night

Silence, the only language she was fluent in
Do you really feel like it was a sin?
Her belief, that so much is said in the unsaid
She never heard your words, but your heart
instead

For some, a prologue
For some, an epilogue
But above all, she was a cosmos of mysteries
She used to heed from the things that usually no
one sees

For her, it was Half Dust Half Deity
For her, every creation was full of creativity
Essence of nature was her friend
Her belief that souls don't but bodies do have an
end

The prettiest artwork,
has the most tragic story to tell
It may be about the obstacles that were conquered
or maybe about some baffling experiences that
were hard to tell

If you want to understand an artist,
you need to know, why her paintings were
demolished
An artist is always reticent, about her feelings
though her artwork is always so revealing

The finest souls are those who gulped pain
though they suffer yet they never complain
Avoid making others taste it,
it's a curse but still they're called gifted

In a room full of people, they disappear
their occult nature was never so clear
I must say, very good in observing people
but observing after an extent, is also lethal

Isn't it too early for you to be judged?
Perhaps one doesn't want to be loved,
so much as to be understood
Either learn the art of expressing yourself, or you're easily misunderstood

Why can't people be more liberal?
They should realize that premature evaluation is also lethal
The whole point of existence was to live carefree
now what will people think, is the reason behind their misery

Eyes hold something,
that words cannot describe
You may not speak a thing,
but your story, is what your eyes will recite

Some avoid eye contact
not wanting their eyes to interact
Not just because they are shy,
but because they know, their eyes will surely reply

And once upon a time
there was girl, for whom cruelty was a crime
The only thing she ever tried to find was kindness
but, oh well! The world is not so selfless

As days went by and she got older
the only thing she realized, people getting colder
Gradually, she started enjoying her own company
even I got flabbergasted, when I saw her rejoicing
in her own agony

Eventually she became the poem I could never
write
a chaotic girl, who suddenly became so quiet
Her life became, Half Exquisite Half Tragic
the girl who always believed in mysteries and
magic

The immense love that I find in early mornings
trees grooving and sky trying to showcase it's
drawings
when a sense of serenity is ignited,
this kind of solitude always made me so excited

In this tranquil, the answers are hidden
an oracle bestowed with cosmic wisdom
When everyone is half asleep half awake
mysteries of nature will always leave you amazed

She was incandescently beautiful,
and beauty was the least of her
She fell in love with the thought of being successful
empathy was her beauty forever

She was so much reticent about her feelings
so reserved, no one knew about her dealings
A part of her, loved writing eulogies about the mighty dead
though very good in reading others, yet she herself was unread.

You'll never be everyone's cup of tea,
because you're a champagne darling
People may get mesmerized by your beauty
the one with charming personality and a warning

Girl, beauty is eternal
the old, the better
beauty is, you being humble
its basically knowing what you need and what
you've to declutter

Beauty is wisdom,
beauty is tremendous grace
It is basically creating your own kingdom,
with elegance that you embrace.

In English we say, I'm tired
but in poetry we say,

Gazing at stars didn't give me the same happiness
anymore
Whispers of wind, didn't ignite that same
excitement anymore
Veins in my arms became weak
Ache in my heart, made it difficult for me to speak
My soul wasn't able to seek refuge
A constant battle between heart and mind, stealing
the very breath from me.

A little bit of peace and tranquil
a few incomplete pages that I was never able to fill
Though alone but never found myself lonely
talking is fine but silence was my kind of glory

Found love in sunflower
and solitude in thunder
writing letters was my kind of thing
emotions on paper for me, was much easier to
bring

Was silent like deep water,
too complex to understand this author
Believed in both aspects of agony and blissful
moments
life for her was, full of mistakes and improvements.

Don't get too close
I'll turn you into a poetry
Chapter of my existence will be easily closed,
But your existence will be eternal through my
poetry

The point here is not to live forever
But to create something that will
The name of the poet you may not remember
forever
But, remembrance of poetry is something
impossible to kill.

Note from the poetess

I don't know what you're thinking after completing this book but I can see that, at some point these poems forced you to introspect.

These poems are very close to me because these are a part of me that I was never able to tell anyone. Many of these poems may force you think that what actually happened and that's what the beauty of literature is; it forces you to think and introspect.

From this collection of poems, I wanted to convey that everyone has their set of ups and downs. These ups and downs will only lead you to your best version.

Why I published this book?

The biggest reason behind publishing this collection of poems was to prove myself wrong. You see, few years back, one of my closest friends told me that I can never learn English by watching English movies or reading books. A part of me believed that person and that was my biggest mistake.

It took me four years to realize, that he was wrong and I was wrong too because I believed him.
You're not what others think or say about you. You're what you think about yourself.

Don't try to be somebody else's perfect.

www.ingramcontent.com/pod-product-compliance
Lightning Source LLC
LaVergne TN
LVHW091239150826
845673LV00003B/1216

* 9 7 9 8 8 9 5 8 8 1 1 2 5 *